Copyright 2012
Revised Format Edition
Golden Eagle, IL

All rights reserved. No part of this publication may be reproduced, stored in a retrieval system or transmitted, in any form without the permission of the author. No title or idea from books in process may be reproduced or used.

A Proverb For EveryDay – Paragraph Format
Revised Format For: Proverbs, Your Monthly Guide For Life
Part of "God's Word For Your Needs" ShortCut Series
By: Wendy R. H. Rose

ISBN 13: 9781480278967
ISBN 10: 1480278963

www.WendyRHRose.net
info@WendyRHRose.net
wendy.r.h.rose@gmail.com

Other books also copyright 2012
www.themoonshines.net
info@themoonshines.net

A PROVERB FOR EVERYDAY –
PARAGRAPH FORMAT

Revised Format for Proverbs, Your Monthly Guide For Life

Part of
"God's Word For Your Needs" ShortCut Series

By Wendy R. H. Rose

Intro to Proverbs
Taken from the Good News Bible,
Today's English Version translation,
American Bible Society 1976

The book of Proverbs is a collection of moral and religious teachings in the form of sayings and proverbs. Much of it has to do with practical, everyday concerns. It begins with the reminder that "To have knowledge, you must first have reverence for the Lord," and then goes onto deal with matters not only of religious morality, but also of common sense and good manners. Its many short sayings reveal the insights of ancient Israelite teachers about what a wise person will do in certain situation. Some of these concern family relations, others, business dealings. Some deal with the matters of etiquette in social relationships, and others with the need of self-control. Much is said about such qualities as humility, patience, respect for the poor, and loyalty to friends.

Outline of Contents:

1:1 – 9:18	In praise of Wisdom
10:1 – 29:27	The proverbs of Solomon
30:1-33	The words of Agur
31:1-31	A capable wife

Intro to Proverbs
Taken from the Contemporary English Version,
American Bible Society 1995

The Book of Proverbs is a collection of sayings that were used in ancient Israel to teach God's people how to live right. For the most part, these sayings to back to Solomon, but others are traced back to Agur and King Lemuel as noted in Chapters 30 and 31 respectively.

Like the Psalms, all the Proverbs are written in poetic form. A typical Proverb takes the form of a short verse in which the first half states the theme and the second half echoes it. What makes the Bible's Proverbs so popular is that they make such powerful statements with very few words. This makes them easy to memorize and apply to daily life.

One of the main teachings in Proverbs is that all wisdom is a gift from God. This wisdom supplies practical advice for everyday living, in the home, in society, in politics, at school, and at work. The Book of Proverbs also teaches the importance of fairness, humility, loyalty, and concern for the poor and needy.

Because most proverbs are so brief, and make their point in one verse, many are often not connected to those around them. In some parts of the book however, a common theme can be found. How not to be a fool is the theme of chapter 16: 1-12, for example. In Chapters 8 and 9, Wisdom is pictured as a woman who advises people to turn from their foolish ways and to live wisely.

A Quick Look at this Book:

1:1-7	Introduction: How Proverbs can be used
1:8 – 7:27	Parental advice on the importance of seeking wisdom and not being foolish
8:1-35	In praise of Wisdom
9:1-18	Wisdom's Feast
10:1-24:34	Solomon's wise sayings
25:1-29:27	More of Solomon's wise sayings
30:1-33	The sayings of Agur
31:1-31	What King Lemuel's mother taught him

Let the words of my mouth and the meditation of my heart be acceptable in Your sight, O Lord, my Rock and my Redeemer
Psalm 19:14

Proverbs has 31 chapters. Start with whatever day of the month it is and read that chapter. Do this several times a year.

Proverbs 1

The proverbs of Solomon, son of David, king of Israel:

The Beginning of Knowledge

To know wisdom and instruction, to understand words of insight, to receive instruction in wise dealing, in righteousness, justice, and equity; to give prudence to the simple, knowledge and discretion to the youth—Let the wise hear and increase in learning, and the one who understands obtain guidance, to understand a proverb and a saying, the words of the wise and their riddles.

The fear of the LORD is the beginning of knowledge; fools despise wisdom and instruction.

Warnings Against Evil Companions

Hear, my son, your father's instruction, and forsake not your mother's teaching, for they are a graceful garland for your head and pendants for your neck.

My son, if sinners entice you, do not consent. If they say, "Come with us, let us lie in wait for blood; let us ambush the innocent without reason; like Sheol let us swallow them alive, and whole, like those who go down to the pit; we shall find all precious goods, we shall fill our houses with plunder; throw in your lot among us; we will all have one purse"—my son, do not walk in the way with them; hold back your foot from their paths, for their feet run to evil, and they make haste to shed blood. For in vain is a net spread in the sight of any bird, but these men lie in wait for their own blood; they set an ambush for their own lives.

Such are the ways of everyone who is greedy for unjust gain; it takes away the life of its possessors.

The Call of Wisdom

Wisdom cries aloud in the street, in the markets she raises her voice; at the head of the noisy streets she cries out; at the entrance of the city gates she speaks: "How long, O simple ones, will you love being simple? How long will scoffers delight in their scoffing and fools hate knowledge? If you turn at my reproof, behold, I will pour out my spirit to you; I will make my words known to you. Because I have called and you refused to listen, have stretched out my hand and no one has heeded, because you have ignored all my counsel and would have none of my reproof, I also will laugh at your calamity; I will mock when terror strikes you, when terror strikes you like a storm and your calamity comes like a whirlwind, when distress and anguish come upon you. Then they will call upon me, but I will not answer; they will seek me diligently but will not find me. Because they hated knowledge and did not choose the fear of the LORD, would have none of my counsel and despised all my reproof, therefore they shall eat the fruit of their way, and have their fill of their own devices. For the simple are killed by their turning away, and the complacency of fools destroys them; but whoever listens to me will dwell secure and will be at ease, without dread of disaster."
(Proverbs 1 ESV)

Date(s) Read:_____

My Thoughts:

Proverbs 2

The Value of Wisdom

My son, if you receive my words and treasure up my commandments with you, making your ear attentive to wisdom and inclining your heart to understanding; yes, if you call out for insight and raise your voice for understanding, if you seek it like silver and search for it as for hidden treasures, then you will understand the fear of the LORD and find the knowledge of God.

For the LORD gives wisdom; from his mouth come knowledge and understanding; he stores up sound wisdom for the upright; he is a shield to those who walk in integrity, guarding the paths of justice and watching over the way of his saints.

Then you will understand righteousness and justice and equity, every good path; for wisdom will come into your heart, and knowledge will be pleasant to your soul; discretion will watch over you, understanding will guard you, delivering you from the way of evil, from men of perverted speech, who forsake the paths of uprightness to walk in the ways of darkness, who rejoice in doing evil and delight in the perverseness of evil, men whose paths are crooked, and who are devious in their ways.

So you will be delivered from the forbidden woman, from the adulteress with her smooth words, who forsakes the companion of her youth and forgets the covenant of her God; for her house sinks down to death, and her paths to the departed; none who go to her come back, nor do they regain the paths of life.

So you will walk in the way of the good and keep to the paths of the righteous. For the upright will inhabit the

land, and those with integrity will remain in it, but the wicked will be cut off from the land, and the treacherous will be rooted out of it.
(Proverbs 2 ESV)

Date(s) Read:_____

My Thoughts:

Proverbs 3

Trust In The Lord With All Your Heart

My son, do not forget my teaching, but let your heart keep my commandments, for length of days and years of life and peace they will add to you. Let not steadfast love and faithfulness forsake you; bind them around your neck; write them on the tablet of your heart. So you will find favor and good success in the sight of God and man.

Trust in the LORD with all your heart, and do not lean on your own understanding. In all your ways acknowledge him, and he will make straight your paths.

Be not wise in your own eyes; fear the LORD, and turn away from evil. It will be healing to your flesh and refreshment to your bones. Honor the LORD with your wealth and with the firstfruits of all your produce; then your barns will be filled with plenty, and your vats will be bursting with wine.

My son, do not despise the LORD's discipline or be weary of his reproof, for the LORD reproves him whom he loves, as a father the son in whom he delights.

Blessed is the One Who Finds Wisdom

Blessed is the one who finds wisdom, and the one who gets understanding, for the gain from her is better than gain from silver and her profit better than gold. She is more precious than jewels, and nothing you desire can compare with her. Long life is in her right hand; in her left hand are riches and honor. Her ways are ways of pleasantness, and all her paths are peace. She is a tree of life to those who lay hold of her; those who hold her fast are called blessed.

God's Wisdom in creation

The LORD by wisdom founded the earth; by understanding he established the heavens; by his knowledge the deeps broke open, and the clouds drop down the dew.

My son, do not lose sight of these—keep sound wisdom and discretion, and they will be life for your soul and adornment for your neck. Then you will walk on your way securely, and your foot will not stumble. If you lie down, you will not be afraid; when you lie down, your sleep will be sweet. Do not be afraid of sudden terror or of the ruin of the wicked, when it comes, for the LORD will be your confidence and will keep your foot from being caught.

Do not withhold good from those to whom it is due, when it is in your power to do it. Do not say to your neighbor, "Go, and come again, tomorrow I will give it"—when you have it with you.

Do not plan evil against your neighbor, who dwells trustingly beside you. Do not contend with a man for no reason, when he has done you no harm. Do not envy a man of violence and do not choose any of his ways, for the devious person is an abomination to the LORD, but the upright are in his confidence.

The LORD's curse is on the house of the wicked, but he blesses the dwelling of the righteous. Toward the scorners he is scornful, but to the humble he gives favor. The wise will inherit honor, but fools get disgrace.
(Proverbs 3 ESV)

Date(s) Read:_____

My Thoughts:

Proverbs 4

Parental Advice

Hear, O sons, a father's instruction, and be attentive, that you may gain insight, for I give you good precepts; do not forsake my teaching. When I was a son with my father, tender, the only one in the sight of my mother, he taught me and said to me, "Let your heart hold fast my words; keep my commandments, and live.

Get wisdom; get insight; do not forget, and do not turn away from the words of my mouth. Do not forsake her, and she will keep you; love her, and she will guard you. The beginning of wisdom is this: Get wisdom, and whatever you get, get insight. Prize her highly, and she will exalt you; she will honor you if you embrace her. She will place on your head a graceful garland; she will bestow on you a beautiful crown.

Admonition to Keep to the Right Path

"Hear, my son, and accept my words, that the years of your life may be many. I have taught you the way of wisdom; I have led you in the paths of uprightness. When you walk, your step will not be hampered, and if you run, you will not stumble. Keep hold of instruction; do not let go;   guard her, for she is your life. Do not enter the path of the wicked, and do not walk in the way of the evil. Avoid it; do not go on it; turn away from it and pass on.

For they cannot sleep unless they have done wrong; they are robbed of sleep unless they have made someone stumble. For they eat the bread of wickedness and drink the wine of violence. But the path of the righteous is like the light of dawn, which shines brighter and brighter until full day. The way of the wicked is like deep darkness; they do not know over what they stumble.

My son, be attentive to my words; incline your ear to my sayings. Let them not escape from your sight; keep them within your heart. For they are life to those who find them, and healing to all their flesh. Keep your heart with all vigilance, for from it flow the springs of life. Put away from you crooked speech, and put devious talk far from you. Let your eyes look directly forward, and your gaze be straight before you. Ponder the path of your feet; then all your ways will be sure.

Do not swerve to the right or to the left; turn your foot away from evil.
(Proverbs 4 ESV)

Date(s) Read:_____

My Thoughts:

Proverbs 5

Warning Against Impurity and Infidelity

My son, be attentive to my wisdom; incline your ear to my understanding, that you may keep discretion, and your lips may guard knowledge. For the lips of a forbidden woman drip honey, and her speech is smoother than oil, but in the end she is bitter as wormwood, sharp as a two-edged sword. Her feet go down to death; her steps follow the path to Sheol; she does not ponder the path of life; her ways wander, and she does not know it.

And now, O sons, listen to me, and do not depart from the words of my mouth. Keep your way far from her, and do not go near the door of her house, lest you give your honor to others and your years to the merciless,

lest strangers take their fill of your strength, and your labors go to the house of a foreigner, and at the end of your life you groan, when your flesh and body are consumed, and you say, "How I hated discipline, and my heart despised reproof!

I did not listen to the voice of my teachers or incline my ear to my instructors. I am at the brink of utter ruin

in the assembled congregation."

Drink water from your own cistern, flowing water from your own well. Should your springs be scattered abroad, streams of water in the streets? Let them be for yourself alone, and not for strangers with you. Let your fountain be blessed, and rejoice in the wife of your youth, a lovely deer, a graceful doe. Let her breasts fill you at all times with delight; be intoxicated always in her love.

Why should you be intoxicated, my son, with a forbidden woman and embrace the bosom of an adulteress?

For a man's ways are before the eyes of the LORD, and he ponders all his paths. The iniquities of the wicked ensnare him, and he is held fast in the cords of his sin. He dies for lack of discipline, and because of his great folly he is led astray.
(Proverbs 5 ESV)

Date(s) Read:_____

My Thoughts:

Proverbs 6

Practical Warnings

My son, if you have put up security for your neighbor, have given your pledge for a stranger, if you are snared in the words of your mouth, caught in the words of your mouth, then do this, my son, and save yourself, for you have come into the hand of your neighbor: go, hasten, and plead urgently with your neighbor.

Give your eyes no sleep and your eyelids no slumber; save yourself like a gazelle from the hand of the hunter, like a bird from the hand of the fowler. Go to the ant, O sluggard; consider her ways, and be wise. Without having any chief, officer, or ruler, she prepares her bread in summer and gathers her food in harvest. How long will you lie there, O sluggard? When will you arise from your sleep? A little sleep, a little slumber, a little folding of the hands to rest, and poverty will come upon you like a robber, and want like an armed man.

A worthless person, a wicked man, goes about with crooked speech, winks with his eyes, signals with his feet, points with his finger, with perverted heart devises evil, continually sowing discord; therefore calamity will come upon him suddenly; in a moment he will be broken beyond healing.

There are six things that the LORD hates, seven that are an abomination to him: haughty eyes, a lying tongue, and hands that shed innocent blood, a heart that devises wicked plans, feet that make haste to run to evil, a false witness who breathes out lies, and one who sows discord among brothers.

Warnings Against Adultery

My son, keep your father's commandment, and forsake not your mother's teaching. Bind them on your heart always; tie them around your neck. When you walk, they will lead you when you lie down, they will watch over you; and when you awake, they will talk with you.

For the commandment is a lamp and the teaching a light, and the reproofs of discipline are the way of life, to preserve you from the evil woman, from the smooth tongue of the adulteress. Do not desire her beauty in your heart, and do not let her capture you with her eyelashes; for the price of a prostitute is only a loaf of bread, but a married woman hunts down a precious life.

Can a man carry fire next to his chest and his clothes not be burned? Or can one walk on hot coals and his feet not be scorched? So is he who goes in to his neighbor's wife; none who touches her will go unpunished.

People do not despise a thief if he steals to satisfy his appetite when he is hungry, but if he is caught, he will pay sevenfold; he will give all the goods of his house.

He who commits adultery lacks sense; he who does it destroys himself. He will get wounds and dishonor, and his disgrace will not be wiped away.

For jealousy makes a man furious, and he will not spare when he takes revenge. He will accept no compensation; he will refuse though you multiply gifts.
(Proverbs 6 ESV)

Date(s) Read:_____

My Thoughts:

Proverbs 7

The False Attractions of Adultery

My son, keep my words and treasure up my commandments with you; keep my commandments and live; keep my teaching as the apple of your eye; bind them on your fingers; write them on the tablet of your heart.

Say to wisdom, "You are my sister," and call insight your intimate friend, to keep you from the forbidden woman, from the adulteress with her smooth words. For at the window of my house I have looked out through my lattice, and I have seen among the simple, I have perceived among the youths, a young man lacking sense, passing along the street near her corner, taking the road to her house in the twilight, in the evening, at the time of night and darkness.

And behold, the woman meets him, dressed as a prostitute, wily of heart. She is loud and wayward; her feet do not stay at home; now in the street, now in the market, and at every corner she lies in wait. She seizes him and kisses him, and with bold face she says to him, "I had to offer sacrifices, and today I have paid my vows; so now I have come out to meet you, to seek you eagerly, and I have found you. I have spread my couch with coverings, colored linens from Egyptian linen; I have perfumed my bed with myrrh, aloes, and cinnamon. Come, let us take our fill of love till morning; let us delight ourselves with love. For my husband is not at home; he has gone on a long journey; he took a bag of money with him; at full moon he will come home." With much seductive speech she persuades him; with her smooth talk she compels him. All at once he follows her, as an ox goes to the slaughter, or as a stag is caught fast till an arrow pierces its liver; as a bird rushes into a snare; he does not know that it will cost him his life.

    And now, O sons, listen to me, and be attentive to the words of my mouth. Let not your heart turn aside to her ways; do not stray into her paths, for many a victim has she laid low, and all her slain are a mighty throng. Her house is the way to Sheol, going down to the chambers of death.
(Proverbs 7 ESV)

Date(s) Read:_____

My Thoughts:

Proverbs 8

The Gifts of Wisdom

Does not wisdom call? Does not understanding raise her voice? On the heights beside the way, at the crossroads she takes her stand; beside the gates in front of the town, at the entrance of the portals she cries aloud: "To you, O men, I call, and my cry is to the children of man .O simple ones, learn prudence; O fools, learn sense.

Hear, for I will speak noble things, and from my lips will come what is right, for my mouth will utter truth; wickedness is an abomination to my lips. All the words of my mouth are righteous; there is nothing twisted or crooked in them. They are all straight to him who understands, and right to those who find knowledge.

Take my instruction instead of silver, and knowledge rather than choice gold, for wisdom is better than jewels, and all that you may desire cannot compare with her.

"I, wisdom, dwell with prudence, and I find knowledge and discretion. The fear of the LORD is hatred of evil. Pride and arrogance and the way of evil and perverted speech I hate. I have counsel and sound wisdom; I have insight; I have strength. By me kings reign, and rulers decree what is just; by me princes rule, and nobles, all who govern justly. I love those who love me, and those who seek me diligently find me. Riches and honor are with me, enduring wealth and righteousness. My fruit is better than gold, even fine gold, and my yield than choice silver. I walk in the way of righteousness, in the paths of justice, granting an inheritance to those who love me, and filling their treasuries.

Wisdom's Part in Creation (see also John's Gospel ch 1:1-18)

"The LORD possessed me at the beginning of his work, the first of his acts of old. Ages ago I was set up, at the first, before the beginning of the earth. When there were no depths I was brought forth, when there were no springs abounding with water. Before the mountains had been shaped, before the hills, I was brought forth, before he had made the earth with its fields, or the first of the dust of the world. When he established the heavens, I was there; when he drew a circle on the face of the deep, when he made firm the skies above, when he established the fountains of the deep, when he assigned to the sea its limit, so that the waters might not transgress his command, when he marked out the foundations of the earth, then I was beside him, like a master workman, and I was daily his delight, rejoicing before him always, rejoicing in his inhabited world and delighting in the children of man.

"And now, O sons, listen to me: blessed are those who keep my ways. Hear instruction and be wise, and do not neglect it. Blessed is the one who listens to me, watching daily at my gates, waiting beside my doors. For whoever finds me finds life   and obtains favor from the LORD, but he who fails to find me injures himself; all who hate me love death." (Proverbs 8 ESV)

Date(s) Read:_____

My Thoughts:

Proverbs 9

Wisdom's Feast

Wisdom has built her house; she has hewn her seven pillars. She has slaughtered her beasts; she has mixed her wine; she has also set her table. She has sent out her young women to call from the highest places in the town, "Whoever is simple, let him turn in here!" To him who lacks sense she says, "Come, eat of my bread and drink of the wine I have mixed. Leave your simple ways, and live, and walk in the way of insight."

General Maxims

Whoever corrects a scoffer gets himself abuse, and he who reproves a wicked man incurs injury. Do not reprove a scoffer, or he will hate you; reprove a wise man, and he will love you. Give instruction to a wise man, and he will be still wiser; teach a righteous man, and he will increase in learning. The fear of the LORD is the beginning of wisdom, and the knowledge of the Holy One is insight. For by me your days will be multiplied, and years will be added to your life. If you are wise, you are wise for yourself; if you scoff, you alone will bear it.

Folly's Invitation and Promise

The woman Folly is loud; she is seductive and knows nothing. She sits at the door of her house; she takes a seat on the highest places of the town, calling to those who pass by, who are going straight on their way, "Whoever is simple, let him turn in here!" And to him who lacks sense she says, "Stolen water is sweet, and bread eaten in secret is pleasant." But he does not know that the dead are there, that her guests are in the depths of Sheol. (Proverbs 9 ESV)

Date(s) Read:_____

My Thoughts:

Proverbs 10

Wise Sayings of Solomon

The proverbs of Solomon. A wise son makes a glad father, but a foolish son is a sorrow to his mother. Treasures gained by wickedness do not profit, but righteousness delivers from death. The LORD does not let the righteous go hungry, but he thwarts the craving of the wicked. A slack hand causes poverty, but the hand of the diligent makes rich. He who gathers in summer is a prudent son, but he who sleeps in harvest is a son who brings shame.

Blessings are on the head of the righteous, but the mouth of the wicked conceals violence. The memory of the righteous is a blessing, but the name of the wicked will rot. The wise of heart will receive commandments, but a babbling fool will come to ruin.

Whoever walks in integrity walks securely, but he who makes his ways crooked will be found out. Whoever winks the eye causes trouble, and a babbling fool will come to ruin. The mouth of the righteous is a fountain of life, but the mouth of the wicked conceals violence.

Hatred stirs up strife, but love covers all offenses. On the lips of him who has understanding, wisdom is found, but a rod is for the back of him who lacks sense. The wise lay up knowledge, but the mouth of a fool brings ruin near. A rich man's wealth is his strong city; the poverty of the poor is their ruin. The wage of the righteous leads to life, the gain of the wicked to sin.

Whoever heeds instruction is on the path to life, but he who rejects reproof leads others astray. The one who conceals hatred has lying lips, and whoever utters slander is a fool.

When words are many, transgression is not lacking, but whoever restrains his lips is prudent. The tongue of the righteous is choice silver; the heart of the wicked is of little worth. The lips of the righteous feed many, but fools die for lack of sense.

The blessing of the LORD makes rich, and he adds no sorrow with it. Doing wrong is like a joke to a fool, but wisdom is pleasure to a man of understanding. What the wicked dreads will come upon him, but the desire of the righteous will be granted. When the tempest passes, the wicked is no more, but the righteous is established forever. Like vinegar to the teeth and smoke to the eyes, so is the sluggard to those who send him. The fear of the LORD prolongs life, but the years of the wicked will be short. The hope of the righteous brings joy, but the expectation of the wicked will perish.

The way of the LORD is a stronghold to the blameless, but destruction to evildoers. The righteous will never be removed, but the wicked will not dwell in the land. The mouth of the righteous brings forth wisdom, but the perverse tongue will be cut off. The lips of the righteous know what is acceptable, but the mouth of the wicked, what is perverse.
(Proverbs 10 ESV)

Date(s) Read:_____

My Thoughts:

Proverbs 11

A false balance is an abomination to the LORD, but a just weight is his delight. When pride comes, then comes disgrace, but with the humble is wisdom. The integrity of the upright guides them, but the crookedness of the treacherous destroys them. Riches do not profit in the day of wrath, but righteousness delivers from death. The righteousness of the blameless keeps his way straight, but the wicked falls by his own wickedness. The righteousness of the upright delivers them, but the treacherous are taken captive by their lust. When the wicked dies, his hope will perish, and the expectation of wealth perishes too. The righteous is delivered from trouble, and the wicked walks into it instead. With his mouth the godless man would destroy his neighbor, but by knowledge the righteous are delivered. When it goes well with the righteous, the city rejoices, and when the wicked perish there are shouts of gladness. By the blessing of the upright a city is exalted, but by the mouth of the wicked it is overthrown.

Whoever belittles his neighbor lacks sense, but a man of understanding remains silent. Whoever goes about slandering reveals secrets, but he who is trustworthy in spirit keeps a thing covered.

Where there is no guidance, a people falls, but in an abundance of counselors there is safety. Whoever puts up security for a stranger will surely suffer harm, but he who hates striking hands in pledge is secure. A gracious woman gets honor, and violent men get riches. A man who is kind benefits himself, but a cruel man hurts himself. The wicked earns deceptive wages, but one who sows righteousness gets a sure reward.

Whoever is steadfast in righteousness will live, but he who pursues evil will die. Those of crooked heart are an abomination to the LORD, but those of blameless ways are his delight. Be assured, an evil person will not go unpunished, but the offspring of the righteous will be delivered.

Like a gold ring in a pig's snout is a beautiful woman without discretion. The desire of the righteous ends only in good; the expectation of the wicked in wrath. One gives freely, yet grows all the richer; another withholds what he should give, and only suffers want.

Whoever brings blessing will be enriched, and one who waters will himself be watered. The people curse him who holds back grain, but a blessing is on the head of him who sells it. Whoever diligently seeks good seeks favor, but evil comes to him who searches for it. Whoever trusts in his riches will fall, but the righteous will flourish like a green leaf. Whoever troubles his own household will inherit the wind, and the fool will be servant to the wise of heart.

The fruit of the righteous is a tree of life, and whoever captures souls is wise. If the righteous is repaid on earth, how much more the wicked and the sinner!
(Proverbs 11 ESV)

Date(s) Read:_____

My Thoughts:

Proverbs 12

Whoever loves discipline loves knowledge, but he who hates reproof is stupid. A good man obtains favor from the LORD, but a man of evil devices he condemns. No one is established by wickedness, but the root of the righteous will never be moved.

An excellent wife is the crown of her husband, but she who brings shame is like rottenness in his bones. The thoughts of the righteous are just; the counsels of the wicked are deceitful. The words of the wicked lie in wait for blood, but the mouth of the upright delivers them. The wicked are overthrown and are no more, but the house of the righteous will stand.

A man is commended according to his good sense, but one of twisted mind is despised. Better to be lowly and have a servant than to play the great man and lack bread. Whoever is righteous has regard for the life of his beast, but the mercy of the wicked is cruel. Whoever works his land will have plenty of bread, but he who follows worthless pursuits lacks sense.

Whoever is wicked covets the spoil of evildoers, but the root of the righteous bears fruit. An evil man is ensnared by the transgression of his lips, but the righteous escapes from trouble. From the fruit of his mouth a man is satisfied with good, and the work of a man's hand comes back to him. The way of a fool is right in his own eyes, but a wise man listens to advice. The vexation of a fool is known at once, but the prudent ignores an insult.

Whoever speaks the truth gives honest evidence, but a false witness utters deceit. There is one whose rash words are like sword thrusts, but the tongue of the wise brings healing. Truthful lips endure forever, but a lying tongue is but for a moment. Deceit is in the heart of those who devise evil, but those who plan peace have joy.

No ill befalls the righteous, but the wicked are filled with trouble. Lying lips are an abomination to the LORD, but those who act faithfully are his delight. A prudent man conceals knowledge, but the heart of fools proclaims folly. The hand of the diligent will rule, while the slothful will be put to forced labor. Anxiety in a man's heart weighs him down, but a good word makes him glad.

One who is righteous is a guide to his neighbor, but the way of the wicked leads them astray.

Whoever is slothful will not roast his game, but the diligent man will get precious wealth. In the path of righteousness is life, and in its pathway there is no death. (Proverbs 12 ESV)

Date(s) Read:_____

My Thoughts:

Proverbs 13

A wise son hears his father's instruction, but a scoffer does not listen to rebuke. From the fruit of his mouth a man eats what is good, but the desire of the treacherous is for violence. Whoever guards his mouth preserves his life; he who opens wide his lips comes to ruin.

The soul of the sluggard craves and gets nothing, while the soul of the diligent is richly supplied. The righteous hates falsehood, but the wicked brings shame and disgrace. Righteousness guards him whose way is blameless, but sin overthrows the wicked.

One pretends to be rich, yet has nothing; another pretends to be poor, yet has great wealth. The ransom of a man's life is his wealth, but a poor man hears no threat. The light of the righteous rejoices, but the lamp of the wicked will be put out. By insolence comes nothing but strife, but with those who take advice is wisdom.

Wealth gained hastily will dwindle, but whoever gathers little by little will increase it. Hope deferred makes the heart sick, but a desire fulfilled is a tree of life. Whoever despises the word brings destruction on himself, but he who reveres the commandment will be rewarded.

The teaching of the wise is a fountain of life, that one may turn away from the snares of death. Good sense wins favor, but the way of the treacherous is their ruin. In everything the prudent acts with knowledge, but a fool flaunts his folly. A wicked messenger falls into trouble, but a faithful envoy brings healing.

Poverty and disgrace come to him who ignores instruction, but whoever heeds reproof is honored. A desire fulfilled is sweet to the soul, but to turn away from evil is an abomination to fools. Whoever walks with the wise becomes wise, but the companion of fools will suffer harm. Disaster pursues sinners, but the righteous are rewarded with good. A good man leaves an inheritance to his children's children, but the sinner's wealth is laid up for the righteous. The fallow ground of the poor would yield much food, but it is swept away through injustice.

Whoever spares the rod hates his son, but he who loves him is diligent to discipline him. The righteous has enough to satisfy his appetite, but the belly of the wicked suffers want.
(Proverbs 13 ESV)

Date(s) Read:_____

My Thoughts:

Proverbs 14

The wisest of women builds her house, but folly with her own hands tears it down. Whoever walks in uprightness fears the LORD, but he who is devious in his ways despises him.

By the mouth of a fool comes a rod for his back, but the lips of the wise will preserve them. Where there are no oxen, the manger is clean, but abundant crops come by the strength of the ox.

A faithful witness does not lie, but a false witness breathes out lies. A scoffer seeks wisdom in vain, but knowledge is easy for a man of understanding. Leave the presence of a fool, for there you do not meet words of knowledge. The wisdom of the prudent is to discern his way, but the folly of fools is deceiving. Fools mock at the guilt offering, but the upright enjoy acceptance.

The heart knows its own bitterness, and no stranger shares its joy.

The house of the wicked will be destroyed, but the tent of the upright will flourish. There is a way that seems right to a man, but its end is the way to death. Even in laughter the heart may ache, and the end of joy may be grief. The backslider in heart will be filled with the fruit of his ways, and a good man will be filled with the fruit of his ways.

The simple believes everything, but the prudent gives thought to his steps. One who is wise is cautious and

turns away from evil, but a fool is reckless and careless.
   A man of quick temper acts foolishly, and a man of evil devices is hated. The simple inherit folly, but the prudent are crowned with knowledge. The evil bow down before the good, the wicked at the gates of the righteous.

   The poor is disliked even by his neighbor, but the rich has many friends. Whoever despises his neighbor is a sinner, but blessed is he who is generous to the poor.

   Do they not go astray who devise evil? Those who devise good meet steadfast love and faithfulness. In all toil there is profit, but mere talk tends only to poverty.

   The crown of the wise is their wealth, but the folly of fools brings folly. A truthful witness saves lives, but one who breathes out lies is deceitful.

   In the fear of the LORD one has strong confidence, and his children will have a refuge. The fear of the LORD is a fountain of life, that one may turn away from the snares of death. In a multitude of people is the glory of a king, but without people a prince is ruined.

   Whoever is slow to anger has great understanding, but he who has a hasty temper exalts folly. A tranquil heart gives life to the flesh, but envy makes the bones rot.

   Whoever oppresses a poor man insults his Maker, but he who is generous to the needy honors him.   The wicked is overthrown through his evildoing, but the righteous finds refuge in his death.

Wisdom rests in the heart of a man of understanding, but it makes itself known even in the midst of fools. Righteousness exalts a nation, but sin is a reproach to any people. A servant who deals wisely has the king's favor, but his wrath falls on one who acts shamefully. (Proverbs 14 ESV)

Date(s) Read:_____

My Thoughts:

Proverbs 15

A soft answer turns away wrath, but a harsh word stirs up anger.

The tongue of the wise commends knowledge, but the mouths of fools pour out folly.

The eyes of the LORD are in every place, keeping watch on the evil and the good. A gentle tongue is a tree of life, but perverseness in it breaks the spirit.

A fool despises his father's instruction, but whoever heeds reproof is prudent. In the house of the righteous there is much treasure, but trouble befalls the income of the wicked. The lips of the wise spread knowledge; not so the hearts of fools. The sacrifice of the wicked is an abomination to the LORD, but the prayer of the upright is acceptable to him. The way of the wicked is an abomination to the LORD, but he loves him who pursues righteousness.

There is severe discipline for him who forsakes the way; whoever hates reproof will die. Sheol and Abaddon lie open before the LORD; how much more the hearts of the children of man! A scoffer does not like to be reproved; he will not go to the wise.

A glad heart makes a cheerful face, but by sorrow of heart the spirit is crushed. The heart of him who has understanding seeks knowledge, but the mouths of fools feed on folly. All the days of the afflicted are evil, but the cheerful of heart has a continual feast.

Better is a little with the fear of the LORD than great treasure and trouble with it. Better is a dinner of herbs where love is than a fattened ox and hatred with it. A hot-tempered man stirs up strife, but he who is slow to anger quiets contention.

The way of a sluggard is like a hedge of thorns, but the path of the upright is a level highway. A wise son makes a glad father, but a foolish man despises his mother.

Folly is a joy to him who lacks sense, but a man of understanding walks straight ahead. Without counsel plans fail, but with many advisers they succeed. To make an apt answer is a joy to a man, and a word in season, how good it is!

The path of life leads upward for the prudent, that he may turn away from Sheol beneath.

The LORD tears down the house of the proud but maintains the widow's boundaries. The thoughts of the wicked are an abomination to the LORD, but gracious words are pure. Whoever is greedy for unjust gain troubles his own household, but he who hates bribes will live.

The heart of the righteous ponders how to answer, but the mouth of the wicked pours out evil things. The LORD is far from the wicked, but he hears the prayer of the righteous. The light of the eyes rejoices the heart, and good news refreshes the bones. The ear that listens to life-giving reproof will dwell among the wise.

Whoever ignores instruction despises himself, but he who listens to reproof gains intelligence. The fear of the LORD is instruction in wisdom, and humility comes before honor. (Proverbs 15 ESV)

Date(s) Read:_____

My Thoughts:

Proverbs 16

The plans of the heart belong to man, but the answer of the tongue is from the LORD. All the ways of a man are pure in his own eyes, but the LORD weighs the spirit.

Commit your work to the LORD, and your plans will be established. The LORD has made everything for its purpose, even the wicked for the day of trouble. Everyone who is arrogant in heart is an abomination to the LORD; be assured, he will not go unpunished.

By steadfast love and faithfulness iniquity is atoned for, and by the fear of the LORD one turns away from evil. When a man's ways please the LORD, he makes even his enemies to be at peace with him.

Better is a little with righteousness than great revenues with injustice. The heart of man plans his way, but the LORD establishes his steps. An oracle is on the lips of a king; his mouth does not sin in judgment. A just balance and scales are the LORD's; all the weights in the bag are his work.

It is an abomination to kings to do evil, for the throne is established by righteousness. Righteous lips are the delight of a king, and he loves him who speaks what is right. A king's wrath is a messenger of death, and a wise man will appease it. In the light of a king's face there is life, and his favor is like the clouds that bring the spring rain. How much better to get wisdom than gold! To get understanding is to be chosen rather than silver.

The highway of the upright turns aside from evil; whoever guards his way preserves his life.

Pride goes before destruction, and a haughty spirit before a fall. It is better to be of a lowly spirit with the poor than to divide the spoil with the proud.

Whoever gives thought to the word will discover good, and blessed is he who trusts in the LORD. The wise of heart is called discerning, and sweetness of speech increases persuasiveness. Good sense is a fountain of life to him who has it, but the instruction of fools is folly. The heart of the wise makes his speech judicious and adds persuasiveness to his lips.

Gracious words are like a honeycomb, sweetness to the soul and health to the body.

There is a way that seems right to a man, but its end is the way to death.

A worker's appetite works for him; his mouth urges him on. A worthless man plots evil, and his speech is like a scorching fire. A dishonest man spreads strife, and a whisperer separates close friends. A man of violence entices his neighbor and leads him in a way that is not good.

Whoever winks his eyes plans dishonest things; he who purses his lips brings evil to pass.

Gray hair is a crown of glory; it is gained in a righteous life.

Whoever is slow to anger is better than the mighty, and he who rules his spirit than he who takes a city. The lot is cast into the lap, but its every decision is from the LORD. (Proverbs 16 ESV)

Date(s) Read:_____

My Thoughts:

Proverbs 17

Better is a dry morsel with quiet than a house full of feasting with strife. A servant who deals wisely will rule over a son who acts shamefully and will share the inheritance as one of the brothers.

The crucible is for silver, and the furnace is for gold, and the LORD tests hearts. An evildoer listens to wicked lips, and a liar gives ear to a mischievous tongue. Whoever mocks the poor insults his Maker; he who is glad at calamity will not go unpunished.

Grandchildren are the crown of the aged, and the glory of children is their fathers. Fine speech is not becoming to a fool; still less is false speech to a prince.

A bribe is like a magic stone in the eyes of the one who gives it; wherever he turns he prospers. Whoever covers an offense seeks love, but he who repeats a matter separates close friends.

A rebuke goes deeper into a man of understanding than a hundred blows into a fool. An evil man seeks only rebellion, and a cruel messenger will be sent against him. Let a man meet a she-bear robbed of her cubs rather than a fool in his folly.

If anyone returns evil for good, evil will not depart from his house. The beginning of strife is like letting out water, so quit before the quarrel breaks out.

He who justifies the wicked and he who condemns the righteous are both alike an abomination to the LORD.

Why should a fool have money in his hand to buy wisdom when he has no sense?

A friend loves at all times, and a brother is born for adversity. One who lacks sense gives a pledge and puts up security in the presence of his neighbor. Whoever loves transgression loves strife; he who makes his door high seeks destruction. A man of crooked heart does not discover good, and one with a dishonest tongue falls into calamity. He who sires a fool gets himself sorrow, and the father of a fool has no joy.

A joyful heart is good medicine, but a crushed spirit dries up the bones. The wicked accepts a bribe in secret to pervert the ways of justice. The discerning sets his face toward wisdom, but the eyes of a fool are on the ends of the earth. A foolish son is a grief to his father and bitterness to her who bore him.

To impose a fine on a righteous man is not good, nor to strike the noble for their uprightness. Whoever restrains his words has knowledge, and he who has a cool spirit is a man of understanding. Even a fool who keeps silent is considered wise; when he closes his lips, he is deemed intelligent. (Proverbs 17 ESV)

Date(s) Read:_____

My Thoughts:

Proverbs 18

Whoever isolates himself seeks his own desire; he breaks out against all sound judgment. A fool takes no pleasure in understanding, but only in expressing his opinion. When wickedness comes, contempt comes also, and with dishonor comes disgrace.

The words of a man's mouth are deep waters; the fountain of wisdom is a bubbling brook. It is not good to be partial to the wicked or to deprive the righteous of justice. A fool's lips walk into a fight, and his mouth invites a beating. A fool's mouth is his ruin, and his lips are a snare to his soul. The words of a whisperer are like delicious morsels; they go down into the inner parts of the body.

Whoever is slack in his work is a brother to him who destroys.

The name of the LORD is a strong tower; the righteous man runs into it and is safe.

A rich man's wealth is his strong city, and like a high wall in his imagination. Before destruction a man's heart is haughty, but humility comes before honor. If one gives an answer before he hears, it is his folly and shame.

A man's spirit will endure sickness, but a crushed spirit who can bear? An intelligent heart acquires knowledge, and the ear of the wise seeks knowledge. A man's gift makes room for him and brings him before the great. The one who states his case first seems right, until the other comes and examines him. The lot puts an end to quarrels and decides between powerful contenders.

A brother offended is more unyielding than a strong city, and quarreling is like the bars of a castle. From the fruit of a man's mouth his stomach is satisfied; he is satisfied by the yield of his lips. Death and life are in the power of the tongue, and those who love it will eat its fruits.

He who finds a wife finds a good thing and obtains favor from the LORD. The poor use entreaties, but the rich answer roughly. A man of many companions may come to ruin, but there is a friend who sticks closer than a brother. (Proverbs 18 ESV)

Date(s) Read:_____

My Thoughts:

Proverbs 19

    Better is a poor person who walks in his integrity than one who is crooked in speech and is a fool. Desire without knowledge is not good, and whoever makes haste with his feet misses his way. When a man's folly brings his way to ruin, his heart rages against the LORD. Wealth brings many new friends, but a poor man is deserted by his friend. A false witness will not go unpunished, and he who breathes out lies will not escape. Many seek the favor of a generous man, and everyone is a friend to a man who gives gifts. All a poor man's brothers hate him; how much more do his friends go far from him! He pursues them with words, but does not have them.

    Whoever gets sense loves his own soul; he who keeps understanding will discover good. A false witness will not go unpunished, and he who breathes out lies will perish. It is not fitting for a fool to live in luxury, much less for a slave to rule over princes.

    Good sense makes one slow to anger, and it is his glory to overlook an offense.

    A king's wrath is like the growling of a lion, but his favor is like dew on the grass. A foolish son is ruin to his father, and a wife's quarreling is a continual dripping of rain. House and wealth are inherited from fathers, but a prudent wife is from the LORD. Slothfulness casts into a deep sleep, and an idle person will suffer hunger.

    Whoever keeps the commandment keeps his life; he who despises his ways will die. Whoever is generous to the poor lends to the LORD, and he will repay him for his deed. Discipline your son, for there is hope; do not set your heart on putting him to death. A man of great wrath will pay the penalty, for if you deliver him, you will only have to do it again. Listen to advice and accept instruction, that you may gain wisdom in the future.

Many are the plans in the mind of a man, but it is the purpose of the LORD that will stand. What is desired in a man is steadfast love, and a poor man is better than a liar. The fear of the LORD leads to life, and whoever has it rests satisfied; he will not be visited by harm.

The sluggard buries his hand in the dish and will not even bring it back to his mouth. Strike a scoffer, and the simple will learn prudence; reprove a man of understanding, and he will gain knowledge.

He who does violence to his father and chases away his mother is a son who brings shame and reproach. Cease to hear instruction, my son, and you will stray from the words of knowledge. A worthless witness mocks at justice, and the mouth of the wicked devours iniquity. Condemnation is ready for scoffers, and beating for the backs of fools. (Proverbs 19 ESV)

Date(s) Read:_____

My Thoughts:

Proverbs 20

Wine is a mocker, strong drink a brawler, and whoever is led astray by it is not wise.

The terror of a king is like the growling of a lion; whoever provokes him to anger forfeits his life. It is an honor for a man to keep aloof from strife, but every fool will be quarreling.

The sluggard does not plow in the autumn; he will seek at harvest and have nothing.

The purpose in a man's heart is like deep water, but a man of understanding will draw it out. Many a man proclaims his own steadfast love, but a faithful man who can find? The righteous who walks in his integrity-blessed are his children after him!

A king who sits on the throne of judgment winnows all evil with his eyes. Who can say, "I have made my heart pure; I am clean from my sin"?

Unequal weights and unequal measures are both alike an abomination to the LORD.

Even a child makes himself known by his acts, by whether his conduct is pure and upright. The hearing ear and the seeing eye, the LORD has made them both. Love not sleep, lest you come to poverty; open your eyes, and you will have plenty of bread. "Bad, bad," says the buyer, but when he goes away, then he boasts.

There is gold and abundance of costly stones, but the lips of knowledge are a precious jewel. Take a man's garment when he has put up security for a stranger, and hold it in pledge when he puts up security for foreigners. Bread gained by deceit is sweet to a man, but afterward his mouth will be full of gravel.

Plans are established by counsel; by wise guidance wage war. Whoever goes about slandering reveals secrets; therefore do not associate with a simple babbler. If one curses his father or his mother, his lamp will be put out in utter darkness. An inheritance gained hastily in the beginning will not be blessed in the end.

Do not say, "I will repay evil"; wait for the LORD, and he will deliver you.

Unequal weights are an abomination to the LORD, and false scales are not good. A man's steps are from the LORD; how then can man understand his way? It is a snare to say rashly, "It is holy," and to reflect only after making vows. A wise king winnows the wicked and drives the wheel over them.

The spirit of man is the lamp of the LORD, searching all his innermost parts. Steadfast love and faithfulness preserve the king, and by steadfast love his throne is upheld. The glory of young men is their strength, but the splendor of old men is their gray hair. Blows that wound cleanse away evil; strokes make clean the innermost parts. (Proverbs 20 ESV)

Date(s) Read:_____

My Thoughts:

Proverbs 21

The king's heart is a stream of water in the hand of the LORD; he turns it wherever he will. Every way of a man is right in his own eyes, but the LORD weighs the heart. To do righteousness and justice is more acceptable to the LORD than sacrifice.

Haughty eyes and a proud heart, the lamp of the wicked, are sin. The plans of the diligent lead surely to abundance, but everyone who is hasty comes only to poverty. The getting of treasures by a lying tongue is a fleeting vapor and a snare of death. The violence of the wicked will sweep them away, because they refuse to do what is just. The way of the guilty is crooked, but the conduct of the pure is upright.

It is better to live in a corner of the housetop than in a house shared with a quarrelsome wife.

The soul of the wicked desires evil; his neighbor finds no mercy in his eyes. When a scoffer is punished, the simple becomes wise; when a wise man is instructed, he gains knowledge. The Righteous One observes the house of the wicked; he throws the wicked down to ruin. Whoever closes his ear to the cry of the poor will himself call out and not be answered.

A gift in secret averts anger, and a concealed bribe, strong wrath. When justice is done, it is a joy to the righteous but terror to evildoers. One who wanders from the way of good sense will rest in the assembly of the dead.

Whoever loves pleasure will be a poor man; he who loves wine and oil will not be rich. The wicked is a ransom for the righteous, and the traitor for the upright.

It is better to live in a desert land than with a quarrelsome and fretful woman.

Precious treasure and oil are in a wise man's dwelling, but a foolish man devours it. Whoever pursues righteousness and kindness will find life, righteousness, and honor. A wise man scales the city of the mighty and brings down the stronghold in which they trust.

Whoever keeps his mouth and his tongue keeps himself out of trouble. "Scoffer" is the name of the arrogant, haughty man who acts with arrogant pride. The desire of the sluggard kills him, for his hands refuse to labor. All day long he craves and craves, but the righteous gives and does not hold back.

The sacrifice of the wicked is an abomination; how much more when he brings it with evil intent. A false witness will perish, but the word of a man who hears will endure. A wicked man puts on a bold face, but the upright gives thought to his ways.

No wisdom, no understanding, no counsel can avail against the LORD. The horse is made ready for the day of battle, but the victory belongs to the LORD.
(Proverbs 21 ESV)

Date(s) Read:_____

My Thoughts:

Proverbs 22

A good name is to be chosen rather than great riches, and favor is better than silver or gold. The rich and the poor meet together; the LORD is the maker of them all.

The prudent sees danger and hides himself, but the simple go on and suffer for it. The reward for humility and fear of the LORD is riches and honor and life. Thorns and snares are in the way of the crooked; whoever guards his soul will keep far from them.

Train up a child in the way he should go; even when he is old he will not depart from it. The rich rules over the poor, and the borrower is the slave of the lender. Whoever sows injustice will reap calamity, and the rod of his fury will fail. Whoever has a bountiful eye will be blessed, for he shares his bread with the poor. Drive out a scoffer, and strife will go out, and quarreling and abuse will cease. He who loves purity of heart, and whose speech is gracious, will have the king as his friend.

The eyes of the LORD keep watch over knowledge, but he overthrows the words of the traitor. The sluggard says, "There is a lion outside! I shall be killed in the streets!" The mouth of forbidden women is a deep pit; he with whom the LORD is angry will fall into it.

Folly is bound up in the heart of a child, but the rod of discipline drives it far from him. Whoever oppresses the poor to increase his own wealth, or gives to the rich, will only come to poverty.

Sayings of The Wise

Incline your ear, and hear the words of the wise, and apply your heart to my knowledge, for it will be pleasant if you keep them within you, if all of them are ready on your lips. That your trust may be in the LORD, I have made them known to you today, even to you.

Have I not written for you thirty sayings of counsel and knowledge, to make you know what is right and true, that you may give a true answer to those who sent you?

Do not rob the poor, because he is poor, or crush the afflicted at the gate, for the LORD will plead their cause and rob of life those who rob them. Make no friendship with a man given to anger, nor go with a wrathful man, lest you learn his ways and entangle yourself in a snare. Be not one of those who give pledges, who put up security for debts. If you have nothing with which to pay, why should your bed be taken from under you? Do not move the ancient landmark that your fathers have set. Do you see a man skillful in his work? He will stand before kings; he will not stand before obscure men.
(Proverbs 22 ESV)

Date(s) Read:_____

My Thoughts:

Proverbs 23

When you sit down to eat with a ruler, observe carefully what is before you, and put a knife to your throat if you are given to appetite. Do not desire his delicacies, for they are deceptive food. Do not toil to acquire wealth; be discerning enough to desist. When your eyes light on it, it is gone, for suddenly it sprouts wings, flying like an eagle toward heaven. Do not eat the bread of a man who is stingy; do not desire his delicacies, for he is like one who is inwardly calculating. "Eat and drink!" he says to you, but his heart is not with you. You will vomit up the morsels that you have eaten, and waste your pleasant words.

Do not speak in the hearing of a fool, for he will despise the good sense of your words. Do not move an ancient landmark or enter the fields of the fatherless, for their Redeemer is strong; he will plead their cause against you.

Apply your heart to instruction and your ear to words of knowledge. Do not withhold discipline from a child; if you strike him with a rod, he will not die. If you strike him with the rod, you will save his soul from Sheol.

My son, if your heart is wise, my heart too will be glad. My inmost being will exult when your lips speak what is right. Let not your heart envy sinners, but continue in the fear of the LORD all the day. Surely there is a future, and your hope will not be cut off. Hear, my son, and be wise, and direct your heart in the way.

Be not among drunkards or among gluttonous eaters of meat, for the drunkard and the glutton will come to poverty, and slumber will clothe them with rags. Listen to your father who gave you life, and do not despise your mother when she is old.

Buy truth, and do not sell it; buy wisdom, instruction, and understanding. The father of the righteous will greatly rejoice; he who fathers a wise son will be glad in him. Let your father and mother be glad; let her who bore you rejoice. My son, give me your heart, and let your eyes observe my ways.

For a prostitute is a deep pit; an adulteress is a narrow well. She lies in wait like a robber and increases the traitors among mankind.

Warnings Against Drunkenness

Who has woe? Who has sorrow? Who has strife? Who has complaining? Who has wounds without cause? Who has redness of eyes? Those who tarry long over wine; those who go to try mixed wine. Do not look at wine when it is red, when it sparkles in the cup and goes down smoothly. In the end it bites like a serpent and stings like an adder. Your eyes will see strange things, and your heart utter perverse things. You will be like one who lies down in the midst of the sea, like one who lies on the top of a mast. "They struck me," you will say, "but I was not hurt; they beat me, but I did not feel it. When shall I awake? I must have another drink."

Date(s) Read:_____

My Thoughts:

Proverbs 24

    Be not envious of evil men, nor desire to be with them, for their hearts devise violence, and their lips talk of trouble. By wisdom a house is built, and by understanding it is established; by knowledge the rooms are filled with all precious and pleasant riches.

    A wise man is full of strength, and a man of knowledge enhances his might, for by wise guidance you can wage your war, and in abundance of counselors there is victory.

    Wisdom is too high for a fool; in the gate he does not open his mouth. Whoever plans to do evil will be called a schemer. The devising of folly is sin, and the scoffer is an abomination to mankind.

    If you faint in the day of adversity, your strength is small. Rescue those who are being taken away to death; hold back those who are stumbling to the slaughter. If you say, "Behold, we did not know this," does not he who weighs the heart perceive it? Does not he who keeps watch over your soul know it, and will he not repay man according to his work?

    My son, eat honey, for it is good, and the drippings of the honeycomb are sweet to your taste. Know that wisdom is such to your soul; if you find it, there will be a future, and your hope will not be cut off. Lie not in wait as a wicked man against the dwelling of the righteous; do no violence to his home; for the righteous falls seven times and rises again, but the wicked stumble in times of calamity.

Do not rejoice when your enemy falls, and let not your heart be glad when he stumbles, lest the LORD see it and be displeased, and turn away his anger from him. Fret not yourself because of evildoers, and be not envious of the wicked, for the evil man has no future; the lamp of the wicked will be put out.

My son, fear the LORD and the king, and do not join with those who do otherwise, for disaster will arise suddenly from them, and who knows the ruin that will come from them both?

More Sayings of the Wise

These also are sayings of the wise. Partiality in judging is not good. Whoever says to the wicked, "You are in the right," will be cursed by peoples, abhorred by nations, but those who rebuke the wicked will have delight, and a good blessing will come upon them.

Whoever gives an honest answer kisses the lips.

Prepare your work outside; get everything ready for yourself in the field, and after that build your house. (Think back to the mistake the settlers of Roanoke, VA made, they were warm but hungry)

Be not a witness against your neighbor without cause, and do not deceive with your lips. Do not say, "I will do to him as he has done to me; I will pay the man back for what he has done."

I passed by the field of a sluggard, by the vineyard of a man lacking sense, and behold, it was all overgrown with thorns; the ground was covered with nettles, and its stone wall was broken down. Then I saw and considered it; I looked and received instruction.

A little sleep, a little slumber, a little folding of the hands to rest, and poverty will come upon you like a robber, and want like an armed man.
(Proverbs 24 ESV)

Date(s) Read:_____

My Thoughts:

Proverbs 25

These also are proverbs of Solomon which the men of Hezekiah king of Judah copied.

It is the glory of God to conceal things, but the glory of kings is to search things out. As the heavens for height, and the earth for depth, so the heart of kings is unsearchable.

Take away the dross from the silver, and the smith has material for a vessel; take away the wicked from the presence of the king, and his throne will be established in righteousness.

Do not put yourself forward in the king's presence or stand in the place of the great, for it is better to be told, "Come up here," than to be put lower in the presence of a noble. (See also Luke 14:10-11 "But when you are invited, go and sit down at the lowest place, so that when your host comes, he may say to you, "Friend, move up higher"; then you will be honored in the presence of all who sit at the table with you. For all who exalt themselves will be humbled, and those who humble themselves will be exalted.")

What your eyes have seen do not hastily bring into court, for what will you do in the end, when your neighbor puts you to shame? Argue your case with your neighbor himself, and do not reveal another's secret, lest he who hears you bring shame upon you, and your ill repute have no end.

A word fitly spoken is like apples of gold in a setting of silver. Like a gold ring or an ornament of gold is a wise reprover to a listening ear.

Like the cold of snow in the time of harvest is a faithful messenger to those who send him; he refreshes the soul of his masters. Like clouds and wind without rain is a man who boasts of a gift he does not give.

With patience a ruler may be persuaded, and a soft tongue will break a bone. If you have found honey, eat only enough for you, lest you have your fill of it and vomit it. Let your foot be seldom in your neighbor's house, lest he have his fill of you and hate you. A man who bears false witness against his neighbor is like a war club, or a sword, or a sharp arrow. Trusting in a treacherous man in time of trouble is like a bad tooth or a foot that slips.

Whoever sings songs to a heavy heart is like one who takes off a garment on a cold day, and like vinegar on soda.

If your enemy is hungry, give him bread to eat, and if he is thirsty, give him water to drink, for you will heap burning coals on his head, and the LORD will reward you.

The north wind brings forth rain, and a backbiting tongue, angry looks. It is better to live in a corner of the housetop than in a house shared with a quarrelsome wife.

Like cold water to a thirsty soul, so is good news from a far country. Like a muddied spring or a polluted fountain is a righteous man who gives way before the wicked. It is not good to eat much honey, nor is it glorious to seek one's own glory.

A man without self-control is like a city broken into and left without walls. (Proverbs 25 ESV)

Date(s) Read:_____

My Thoughts:

Proverbs 26

Like snow in summer or rain in harvest, so honor is not fitting for a fool. Like a sparrow in its flitting, like a swallow in its flying, a curse that is causeless does not alight. A whip for the horse, a bridle for the donkey, and a rod for the back of fools.

Answer not a fool according to his folly, lest you be like him yourself. Answer a fool according to his folly, lest he be wise in his own eyes.

Whoever sends a message by the hand of a fool cuts off his own feet and drinks violence. Like a lame man's legs, which hang useless, is a proverb in the mouth of fools. Like one who binds the stone in the sling is one who gives honor to a fool. Like a thorn that goes up into the hand of a drunkard is a proverb in the mouth of fools. Like an archer who wounds everyone s one who hires a passing fool or drunkard.

Like a dog that returns to his vomit is a fool who repeats his folly. Do you see a man who is wise in his own eyes? There is more hope for a fool than for him. The sluggard says, "There is a lion in the road! There is a lion in the streets!"

As a door turns on its hinges, so does a sluggard on his bed. The sluggard buries his hand in the dish; it wears him out to bring it back to his mouth. The sluggard is wiser in his own eyes than seven men who can answer sensibly.

Whoever meddles in a quarrel not his own is like one who takes a passing dog by the ears.

Like a madman who throws firebrands, arrows, and death is the man who deceives his neighbor and says, "I am only joking!" For lack of wood the fire goes out, and where there is no whisperer, quarreling ceases. As charcoal to hot embers and wood to fire, so is a quarrelsome man for kindling strife. The words of a whisperer are like delicious morsels; they go down into the inner parts of the body.

Like the glaze covering an earthen vessel are fervent lips with an evil heart. Whoever hates disguises himself with his lips and harbors deceit in his heart; when he speaks graciously, believe him not, for there are seven abominations in his heart; though his hatred be covered with deception, his wickedness will be exposed in the assembly. Whoever digs a pit will fall into it, and a stone will come back on him who starts it rolling. A lying tongue hates its victims, and a flattering mouth works ruin. (Proverbs 26 ESV)

Date(s) Read:_____

My Thoughts:

Proverbs 27

Do not boast about tomorrow, for you do not know what a day may bring.

Let another praise you, and not your own mouth; a stranger, and not your own lips.

A stone is heavy, and sand is weighty, but a fool's provocation is heavier than both.

Wrath is cruel, anger is overwhelming, but who can stand before jealousy?

Better is open rebuke than hidden love. Faithful are the wounds of a friend; profuse are the kisses of an enemy. One who is full loathes honey, but to one who is hungry everything bitter is sweet.

Like a bird that strays from its nest is a man who strays from his home. Oil and perfume make the heart glad, and the sweetness of a friend comes from his earnest counsel.

Do not forsake your friend and your father's friend, and do not go to your brother's house in the day of your calamity. Better is a neighbor who is near than a brother who is far away.

Be wise, my son, and make my heart glad, that I may answer him who reproaches me. The prudent sees danger and hides himself, but the simple go on and suffer for it.

Take a man's garment when he has put up security for a stranger, and hold it in pledge when he puts up security for an adulteress. Whoever blesses his neighbor with a loud voice, rising early in the morning, will be counted as cursing.

A continual dripping on a rainy day and a quarrelsome wife are alike; to restrain her is to restrain the wind or to grasp oil in one's right hand.

Iron sharpens iron, and one man sharpens another. Whoever tends a fig tree will eat its fruit, and he who guards his master will be honored.

As in water face reflects face, so the heart of man reflects the man. Sheol and Abaddon are never satisfied, and never satisfied are the eyes of man.

The crucible is for silver, and the furnace is for gold, and a man is tested by his praise. Crush a fool in a mortar with a pestle along with crushed grain, yet his folly will not depart from him. Know well the condition of your flocks, and give attention to your herds, for riches do not last forever; and does a crown endure to all generations?

When the grass is gone and the new growth appears and the vegetation of the mountains is gathered, the lambs will provide your clothing, and the goats the price of a field. There will be enough goats' milk for your food, for the food of your household and maintenance for your girls. (Proverbs 27 ESV)

Date(s) Read:_____

My Thoughts:

Proverbs 28

The wicked flee when no one pursues, but the righteous are bold as a lion.

When a land transgresses, it has many rulers, but with a man of understanding and knowledge, its stability will long continue. A poor man who oppresses the poor is a beating rain that leaves no food. Those who forsake the law praise the wicked, but those who keep the law strive against them.

Evil men do not understand justice, but those who seek the LORD understand it completely. Better is a poor man who walks in his integrity than a rich man who is crooked in his ways. The one who keeps the law is a son with understanding, but a companion of gluttons shames his father.

Whoever multiplies his wealth by interest and profit gathers it for him who is generous to the poor. If one turns away his ear from hearing the law, even his prayer is an abomination. Whoever misleads the upright into an evil way will fall into his own pit, but the blameless will have a goodly inheritance.

A rich man is wise in his own eyes, but a poor man who has understanding will find him out. When the righteous triumph, there is great glory, but when the wicked rise, people hide themselves. Whoever conceals his transgressions will not prosper, but he who confesses and forsakes them will obtain mercy.

Blessed is the one who fears the LORD always, but whoever hardens his heart will fall into calamity. Like a roaring lion or a charging bear is a wicked ruler over a poor people. A ruler who lacks understanding is a cruel oppressor, but he who hates unjust gain will prolong his days.

If one is burdened with the blood of another, he will be a fugitive until death; let no one help him. Whoever walks in integrity will be delivered, but he who is crooked in his ways will suddenly fall. Whoever works his land will have plenty of bread, but he who follows worthless pursuits will have plenty of poverty.

A faithful man will abound with blessings, but whoever hastens to be rich will not go unpunished. To show partiality is not good, but for a piece of bread a man will do wrong. A stingy man hastens after wealth and does not know that poverty will come upon him.

Whoever rebukes a man will afterward find more favor than he who flatters with his tongue. Whoever robs his father or his mother and says, "That is no transgression," is a companion to a man who destroys. A greedy man stirs up strife, but the one who trusts in the LORD will be enriched.

Whoever trusts in his own mind is a fool, but he who walks in wisdom will be delivered. Whoever gives to the poor will not want, but he who hides his eyes will get many a curse. When the wicked rise, people hide themselves, but when they perish, the righteous increase.

Date(s) Read:_____

My Thoughts:

Proverbs 29

He who is often reproved, yet stiffens his neck, will suddenly be broken beyond healing. When the righteous increase, the people rejoice, but when the wicked rule, the people groan. He who loves wisdom makes his father glad, but a companion of prostitutes squanders his wealth.

By justice a king builds up the land, but he who exacts gifts tears it down. A man who flatters his neighbor spreads a net for his feet. An evil man is ensnared in his transgression, but a righteous man sings and rejoices. A righteous man knows the rights of the poor; a wicked man does not understand such knowledge. Scoffers set a city aflame, but the wise turn away wrath.

If a wise man has an argument with a fool, the fool only rages and laughs, and there is no quiet. Bloodthirsty men hate one who is blameless and seek the life of the upright.

A fool gives full vent to his spirit, but a wise man quietly holds it back.

If a ruler listens to falsehood, all his officials will be wicked. The poor man and the oppressor meet together; the LORD gives light to the eyes of both. If a king faithfully judges the poor, his throne will be established forever. The rod and reproof give wisdom, but a child left to himself brings shame to his mother.

When the wicked increase, transgression increases, but the righteous will look upon their downfall.

Discipline your son, and he will give you rest; he will give delight to your heart.

Where there is no prophetic vision the people cast off restraint, but blessed is he who keeps the law. By mere words a servant is not disciplined, for though he understands, he will not respond.

Do you see a man who is hasty in his words? There is more hope for a fool than for him.

Whoever pampers his servant from childhood will in the end find him his heir. A man of wrath stirs up strife, and one given to anger causes much transgression. One's pride will bring him low, but he who is lowly in spirit will obtain honor. The partner of a thief hates his own life; he hears the curse, but discloses nothing. The fear of man lays a snare, but whoever trusts in the LORD is safe. Many seek the face of a ruler, but it is from the LORD that a man gets justice. An unjust man is an abomination to the righteous, but one whose way is straight is an abomination to the wicked. (Proverbs 29 ESV)

Date(s) Read:_____

My Thoughts:

Proverbs 30

Sayings of Agur
    The words of Agur son of Jakeh. The oracle.

    The man declares, I am weary, O God; I am weary, O God, and worn out. Surely I am too stupid to be a man. I have not the understanding of a man. I have not learned wisdom, nor have I knowledge of the Holy One. Who has ascended to heaven and come down? Who has gathered the wind in his fists? Who has wrapped up the waters in a garment? Who has established all the ends of the earth? What is his name, and what is his son's name? Surely you know!

    Every word of God proves true; he is a shield to those who take refuge in him. Do not add to his words, lest he rebuke you and you be found a liar.

    Two things I ask of you; deny them not to me before I die: Remove far from me falsehood and lying; give me neither poverty nor riches; feed me with the food that is needful for me, lest I be full and deny you and say, "Who is the LORD?" or lest I be poor and steal and profane the name of my God.

    Do not slander a servant to his master, lest he curse you, and you be held guilty. There are those who curse their fathers and do not bless their mothers. There are those who are clean in their own eyes but are not washed of their filth. There are those—how lofty are their eyes, how high their eyelids lift! There are those whose teeth are swords, whose fangs are knives, to devour the poor from off the earth, the needy from among mankind.

The leech has two daughters: Give and Give.

Three things are never satisfied; four never say, "Enough": Sheol, the barren womb, the land never satisfied with water, and the fire that never says, "Enough." The eye that mocks a father and scorns to obey a mother will be picked out by the ravens of the valley and eaten by the vultures.

Three things are too wonderful for me; four I do not understand: the way of an eagle in the sky, the way of a serpent on a rock, the way of a ship on the high seas, and the way of a man with a virgin. This is the way of an adulteress: she eats and wipes her mouth and says, "I have done no wrong."

Under three things the earth trembles; under four it cannot bear up: a slave when he becomes king, and a fool when he is filled with food; an unloved woman when she gets a husband, and a maidservant when she displaces her mistress.

Four things on earth are small, but they are exceedingly wise: the ants are a people not strong, yet they provide their food in the summer; the rock badgers are a people not mighty, yet they make their homes in the cliffs; the locusts have no king, yet all of them march in rank; the lizard you can take in your hands, yet it is in kings' palaces.

Three things are stately in their tread; four are stately in their stride: the lion, which is mightiest among beasts and does not turn back before any; the strutting rooster, the he-goat, and a king whose army is with him.

If you have been foolish, exalting yourself, or if you have been devising evil, put your hand on your mouth. For pressing milk produces curds, pressing the nose produces blood, and pressing anger produces strife. (Proverbs 30 ESV)

Date(s) Read:_____

My Thoughts:

Proverbs 31

The Teachings of King Lemuel's Mother

The words of King Lemuel. An oracle that his mother taught him:

What are you doing, my son? What are you doing, son of my womb? What are you doing, son of my vows? Do not give your strength to women, your ways to those who destroy kings. It is not for kings, O Lemuel, it is not for kings to drink wine, or for rulers to take strong drink, lest they drink and forget what has been decreed and pervert the rights of all the afflicted. Give strong drink to the one who is perishing, and wine to those in bitter distress; let them drink and forget their poverty and remember their misery no more. Open your mouth for the mute, for the rights of all who are destitute. Open your mouth, judge righteously, defend the rights of the poor and needy.

Date(s) Read:_____

My Thoughts:

Proverbs 31: Ode To A Capable Wife

An excellent wife who can find?

She is far more precious than jewels. The heart of her husband trusts in her, and he will have no lack of gain. She does him good, and not harm, all the days of her life.

She seeks wool and flax, and works with willing hands. She is like the ships of the merchant; she brings her food from afar. She rises while it is yet night and provides food for her household and portions for her maidens.

She considers a field and buys it; with the fruit of her hands she plants a vineyard. She dresses herself with strength and makes her arms strong.

She perceives that her merchandise is profitable. Her lamp does not go out at night. She puts her hands to the distaff, and her hands hold the spindle. She opens her hand to the poor and reaches out her hands to the needy.

She is not afraid of snow for her household, for all her household are clothed in scarlet. She makes bed coverings for herself; her clothing is fine linen and purple.

Her husband is known in the gates when he sits among the elders of the land.

She makes linen garments and sells them; she delivers sashes to the merchant.

Strength and dignity are her clothing, and she laughs at the time to come. She opens her mouth with wisdom, and the teaching of kindness is on her tongue.

She looks well to the ways of her household and does not eat the bread of idleness.

Her children rise up and call her blessed; her husband also, and he praises her: "Many women have done excellently, but you surpass them all."

Charm is deceitful, and beauty is vain, but a woman who fears the LORD is to be praised. Give her of the fruit of her hands, and let her works praise her in the gates. (Proverbs 31 ESV)

Date(s) Read:_____

My Thoughts:

Other Books to come from Wendy:

God's Law, The 10 Commandments – Do They Still Apply in Modern Times

Be Angry, And Do Not Sin

Bible 365, Daily Reader

Blessed Are, You Really Do Have Good Things In Your Life

Blessings Galore, How It All Works Out

Child / Parent – Ours and Their Responsibility

Fruit of the Spirit, Keep It Fresh and Renewed

Lord's Prayer – First and Final Prayer, Yesterday, Today, and Tomorrow

Prayer – Your Heart to God's Heart

Satan –The Father of All Lies, Who He Is and What He Does

Speech – Why What We Say Kills Us and How To Bring Back The Life God Has For Us

Wives and Husbands, Now and Forever. It's harder than you think. What does marriage really take?

52 Words of Wisdom for the New Bride and Groom

Work Ethics – Why We Succeed or Fail

Books Available
by Wendy R. H. Rose

www.createspace.com
Available on Amazon.com in paperback and on Kindle

Go to www.WendyRHRose.net to order

Hope, What you live for, Your Path to God's will for your life
October 2012
Part of "God's Word For Your Needs" ShortCut Series

A Proverb For Every Day, Paragraph Format
With journaling page

Proverbs, Your Monthly Guide to Life
Verse Format with Journaling page
November 2012
Part of "God's Word For Your Needs" ShortCut Series

Greetings And Benedictions, How To Greet Others In Your Writing
November 2012
Part of "God's Word For Your Needs" ShortCut Series

Copyright 2012   No title or idea from books in process may be reproduced or used.
Other books also copyright 2012
www.wendyrhrose.net
www.themoonshines.net
info@wendyrhrose.net

THE CHURCH YEAR

The Time of Christmas
Advent
4 Sundays
Christmas – The Birth of our Lord
Epiphany (12 days after Christmas)
1st Sunday after Epiphany (Baptism of Our Lord)
2-8 Sunday after Epiphany
Last Sunday after Epiphany (Transfiguration of Our Lord)

Lent
Ash Wednesday is the first day of Lent. It falls in the seventh week before Easter
5 Sundays in Lent
Holy Week
Palm Sunday - Jesus' Entry into Jerusalem
Maundy Thursday - institution of the Lord's Supper and Jesus Arrest
Good Friday – Jesus Crucifixion
Easter Day – Resurrection of Our Lord
Easter is always the Sunday after the full moon that occurs on or after the spring equinox (Mar 21).
Easter Day cannot be earlier than March 22 or later than April 25th.
7 Sundays of Easter

The Ascension of Our Lord occurs on a Thursday, 40 days after Easter Day
The Day of Pentecost The Holy Spirit coming to the disciples and giving them tongues
Pentecost is 7 weeks or the 50th day after Easter
Holy Trinity
Ordinary Time or the rest of the Sundays till Advent

RESOURCES

The Lord's Word and His Daily Inspiration
Lutheran Study Bible, Concordia Publishing House 2009
Lutheran Service Book, Hymnal Concordia Publishing House, 2006
Luther's Small Catechism

Pastor Reuben Ankney, St. Matthew Lutheran Church, Brussels, IL
Pastor William Schmidt, Retired Pastor from Marion and Carrolton, IL
Pastor Gary McCraken, Trinity, Troy, MO
Pastor Matthew Gehrke, Concordia Church, Cottage Hills, IL
Pastor Gray, Our Savior, Carbondale, IL

Bible Translations

ESV English Standard Version
KJV King James Version
NRSV New Revised Standard Version
TEV Today's English Version
CEV Contemporary English Version

My Favorite Passages and What They Mean To Me

Made in the USA
Charleston, SC
16 November 2012